THE
RED SOX
CENTURY

THE
RED SOX
CENTURY

VOICES AND MEMORIES
FROM FENWAY PARK

ALAN ROSS

Cumberland House
Nashville, Tennessee

Copyright © 2004 by Alan Ross

Published by
Cumberland House Publishing, Inc.
431 Harding Industrial Drive
Nashville, TN 37211-3160

Cover design: Gore Studio, Inc., Nashville, Tennessee
Text design: John Mitchell

Library of Congress Cataloging-in-Publication Data

Ross, Alan, 1944-
  The Red Sox century : voices and memories from Fenway Park /
Alan Ross.
      p. cm.
  Includes bibliographical references and index.
  ISBN 1-58182-384-3 (pbk. : alk. paper)
  1. Boston Red Sox (Baseball team)—Anecdotes. 2. Fenway Park
(Boston, Mass.)—Anecdotes. 3. Baseball players—United States—
Anecdotes. I. Title.
  GV875.B7R69 2004
  796.357'64'0974461—dc22

Printed in the United States of America

  2 3 4 5 6 7—10 09 08 07 06 05 04

For Karol,
the memory of my brother Bob,
and the hallowed ground
that is Fenway

Babe Ruth's trade to New York after the 1919 season marked the beginning of The Curse.

CONTENTS

INTRODUCTION

THE RED SOX CENTURY tells the full story of Boston Red Sox baseball, from 1903 to the present, through the voices of its players, managers, opponents, and the media. Though the Sox' tale of modern times mostly seems a struggle of falling just short, it is the Hub's Hose, to quote early Beantown accounts of the club, which dominated the embryonic days of not only the American League but World Series play. Of the first 15 Series, which began in 1903, the Red Sox (né Pilgrims) claimed five crowns.

Everyone remembers the flurries of hope that dotted the mid- to late 1940s, 1967, 1975, 1978, 1986, and most recently, 2003—seasons around which the definition of heartbreak was written. But doesn't it say something stout and resolute about New Englanders, who year after year return to support with passion the Olde Towne Team? For Red Sox fans, weary of failure and broken dreams, hope will always simmer. As former Bosox manager John McNamara once said: "What can you say? You know what the poets say: 'Hope springs eternal in the human breast.'"

REMEMBRANCE

ON SATURDAY, APRIL 27, 1957, a daring 12-year-old steeled his courage to make a dash by the foreboding phalanx of Redcoats. No, there was no presence of British militia, just that stern congregation of old fuzzy-mitten bearers who take spectators to their seats at ballparks and dust the depressed wooden slats where derrieres will soon be deposited. For a small stipend, of course. Beyond that seemingly impregnable red wall, the object of my quest came loping toward the visitors' dugout at Yankee Stadium from the outfield at the end of pregame warm-ups.

My breath quickened. Now was the time. Brownie Holiday camera in hand, I stormed past the front line of Redcoats, who were taken off guard, momentarily stunned by my boldness. It was just enough. In seconds I was at the end of the aisle that dead-ended into the rear of the dugout, leaning far forward to record the Splendid Splinter just as he made his way into the visitors' recess.

Ted Williams, then 38 and in his 16th season with the Red Sox, was still cranking it out. He would lead the league in hitting with a phenomenal .388 average, second only to his milestone .406 in 1941. And there I was, just six feet from him, a living god. The Sox took an early 2–1 lead that afternoon and the score held up, as Sox pitcher Tom Brewer gained his first victory over the Yankees in eight tries over four seasons. The Thumper went 1–for–3, singling in the first Boston run in the top of the first.

That hard-earned photo, reprinted here, remains a treasure from long ago of my initial introduction to the Red Sox and to the man who embodied the brilliant in baseball, as close as a mere mortal could get to the majesty of a Perseus or Poseidon.

ALAN ROSS

THE
RED SOX
CENTURY

RED SOX TRADITION

IT'S ABOUT TRADITION. You think about all the great players that ever played there. . . . Can you imagine taking a sleeping bag to Fenway Park and staying there at night and having the ghosts come and visit you? Just think of all the great players that played left field. And all the great games. That's what this game is all about.

Jim Palmer
Hall of Fame pitcher,
Baltimore Orioles (1965–84)

The Curse of the Bambino is a handy expression for all the woes endured by the Sox and their fans over the last three-quarters of a century. The Curse helps us explain the unexplainable. It's superstition over science, a tidy excuse for Johnny Pesky holding the ball in '46, and Luis Aparicio falling down in '72, and Jim Burton in '75, and Bucky Dent in '78, and Bill Buckner in '86. The Curse is part of Boston folklore and serves to soothe citizens of the Red Sox Nation when bad things happen to good teams.

Dan Shaughnessy
sports journalist/author

The former bare-knuckle fighter was a pioneer of the game of baseball. He set up the first minor league night game in 1896, promoted the only woman ever to pitch in organized baseball (Lizzie Arlington, in 1897), was the first man to paint distances on outfield fences, discovered Honus Wagner, and switched Babe Ruth to the outfield. He also served as general manager and president of the New York Yankees from 1921 to 1945, masterminding them to 14 flags and 10 world championships. . . . He was elected to the Hall of Fame in 1953.

**Ty Waterman and
Mel Springer**

*authors,
on Red Sox manager
Ed Barrow (1918–20)*

We will play not because we think we are getting a fair deal . . . but for the sake of the game, for the sake of the public, which has always given us its loyal support, and for the sake of the wounded soldiers and sailors who are in the grandstand waiting for us.

Harry Hooper

Hall of Fame outfielder (1909-20), the day the Red Sox and Chicago Cubs went on strike, before Game 5 of the 1918 World Series, for a better cut of the Series pay

Umpires made more than the players, earning $1,000 each. Player shares for the winning Red Sox were less than $900.

In 1925, Harry Frazee—by then ex-owner of the Red Sox—had a monster Broadway hit with the musical *No, No, Nanette*. At one point there were five road companies crisscrossing the country singing "Tip-Toe Through the Tulips." Had *Nanette* been written just a half-dozen years earlier, Red Sox fans might have been spared a ton of grief.

David S. Neft, Michael L. Neft, Bob Carroll, and Richard M. Cohen
authors,
on the fateful sale of Babe Ruth after the 1919 season

Ruth's 29 homers were more spectacular than useful; they didn't help the Red Sox get out of sixth place.

> **Harry Frazee**
> *on trading Babe Ruth to the Yankees, 1920*

Boston has two seasons: August and winter.

> **Billy Herman**
> *Red Sox manager (1964–66)*

An almost inexorable law: A Red Sox ship with a single leak will always find a way to sink.

> **Thomas Boswell**
> *sportswriter/author*

You'd think the law of averages would sort of even out—that they would win one.

> **Bobby Doerr**
> *Hall of Fame*
> *second baseman*
> *(1937–44, 1946–51)*

Everything goes against the Red Sox. They're star-crossed lovers in a sense. The wrong thing always happens to the Red Sox.

> **Lou Gorman**
> *Red Sox general manager*
> *(1984–93)*

The *what ifs* cascade upon the mind like raindrops on a field of seedlings giving bloom to a thousand radiant imaginings. What if Buckner makes the play at first? What if Piniella doesn't come up with Remy's drive to right? What if Doyle turns the double-play on Bench? What if Aparicio doesn't slip rounding third? What if it rains and Lonborg gets another day of rest? What if Pesky doesn't hold the ball? What if The Kid never goes to Korea? What if Frazee doesn't sell The Babe?

Dan Riley
editor/writer

Look at...the succession of ridiculous events that symbolized the kind of team we were: the game we hit into six double plays, or one in which we struck out 17 times, five seasons without a 20-game winner, a crowd of 461 for a Fenway home game, a season's record of 1–17 against the Twins . . . and these followed close-but-no-cigar finishes when the team really was good, when it had Ted Williams and Bobby Doerr and Johnny Pesky and Mel Parnell and Ellis Kinder. Good teams, bad teams—it never seemed to matter up in Boston. The Sox always found a way to blow it.

Carl Yastrzemski
*Hall of Fame outfielder
(1961–83), on the Boston
legacy before the
Impossible Dream season
of 1967*

Boston fans are experts at predicting disaster. They should be nationalized to predict earthquakes and hurricanes and tornados, particularly in October.

George Vecsey
columnist,
The New York Times

This was a victory for the underdog; a victory for a city that didn't think it had one left in it.

Carl Yastrzemski
*on clinching the American
League pennant in 1967*

The only real game in the world is baseball.

Babe Ruth

2

RED SOX PRIDE

THE RED SOX are a religion. Every year we reenact the Agony and the Temptation in the Garden. Baseball child's play? Hell, up here in Boston it's a passion play.

George V. Higgins
Time, *1980*

Baseball isn't a life-and-death matter, but the Red Sox are.

Mike Barnicle
The Boston Globe, *1977*

The Yankees belong to George Steinbrenner and the Dodgers belong to Manifest Destiny, but the Red Sox, more than any other team, belong to the fans.

Steve Wulf
Sports Illustrated, *1981*

My clearest memory comes from my youngest son, Owen. In '86 he was nine, and he came down for the third game of the World Series. Oil Can Boyd pitched the game and we lost. . . . As we left the ballpark he started to cry. I said, "Now you're a Red Sox fan."

Stephen King
best-selling novelist

No team is worshiped with such a perverse sense of fatality.

Thomas Boswell
on the Red Sox

It doesn't matter. If they want to cheer me, that's fine. If they want to boo me, that's fine. My fans are in Boston now, so I have nothing to worry about.

Manny Ramirez
outfielder (2001–),
on his eight seasons in
Cleveland before joining
the Red Sox

That night I said to someone, "I think I love Boston already."

Pedro Martinez
pitcher (1998–),
on being greeted at
Boston's airport by hun-
dreds of fans after his
Nov. 18, 1997, trade from
the Montreal Expos to
the Red Sox

I know I'm going to live long enough when we're gonna be world champions.

Johnny Pesky
shortstop (1942, 1946–52)

I just want to win as a team. That's my only challenge left. That's my pride.

Pedro Martinez

We are not losers. The Cubs are losers. We are perennial bridesmaids.

Ethel Crotteau
longtime Boston fan

THE RED AND BLUE

THE WAY TO GET a ball player, to my way of thinking, is to buy him. Money talks louder than newspaper chatter.

Harry Frazee
Red Sox owner and president
(1916–23)

Dwarfing by comparison the famous sale of Tris Speaker two years ago, President Harry Frazee put through the most sensational deal in the history of baseball yesterday when he purchased pitcher "Bullet" Joe Bush, catcher Wally Schang, and outfielder Amos Strunk from the Philadelphia Athletics, surrendering in exchange $60,000 in cash and handing over catcher Chester Thomas, pitcher Vean Gregg, and outfielder Merlin Kopp.

Paul H. Shannon
The Boston Post,
December 15, 1918

Tris Speaker

An hour after I gave Connie Mack $60,000 for the three players—and that was the price—[Chicago White Sox owner Charles] Comiskey offered me $50,000 for Joe Bush alone.

Harry Frazee

In that dead-ball era an outfielder could play shallower than they do today, but Tris Speaker played so shallow that he was able on occasion to turn in unassisted double plays and get involved in rundowns.

Donald Honig
author

Morris Berg is a living antithesis of the Ring Lardner "dumb" ball player. He is baseball's foremost man of letters and his reputation as a scholar is not confined to the diamond world. . . . He doesn't flaunt his knowledge and doesn't like to be classified as linguist or lawyer or a lover of classical music. Instead he likes being called a baseball player.

The New York Times
January 15, 1942

He could speak eight languages, but he couldn't hit in any of them.

Ted Lyons

Twenty-one-year Chicago White Sox pitcher, on Red Sox catcher Moe Berg (1935–39)

The guy's got a fault? Dandruff, maybe.

Leo Durocher

Hall of Fame Giants manager, on Frank Malzone, Red Sox third baseman (1955–65)

Jimmy Piersall squirted home plate with water pistols, heaved equipment bags out of dugouts, watered down the infield between innings, ran into walls trying to catch fly balls, threw baseballs at scoreboards and bats at pitchers, practiced sliding during batting practice, slept on the clubhouse floor, bunted with two out and his team six runs behind in the last of the ninth, ran around the bases backward after hitting homers, did sitting up exercises in the outfield to distract batters, had nervous breakdowns, made comebacks, fathered nine children, and was portrayed by Anthony Perkins in the 1957 movie version of his life story.

**Brendan C. Boyd and
Fred C. Harris**
authors

One of the most exciting players on the team was center fielder Jimmy Piersall, whose career almost ended in his rookie year of 1952. The Red Sox tried to turn Piersall into a short-stop. He began exhibiting bizarre behavior on the field and eventually was sent to the minors, where the problems continued. Eventually it was discovered that he had suffered a complete nervous breakdown. He had no memory of the preceding months or his odd conduct. Happily, he recovered, became a brilliant center fielder and sharp hitter, and was even able to write about his experience in the best-selling book *Fear Strikes Out*.

David S. Neft, Michael L. Neft, Bob Carroll, and Richard M. Cohen

I can still remember the oversized headline in the Boston newspapers and the feeling of stunned incredulity it aroused in all of us—our first encounter with the underlying frailty of the human condition. Up until then death had been something that only happened to animals or in the movies or to bank robbers or people who had fires in their houses or to the old. But Harry Agganis? If something like this could happen to Harry Agganis, then what was to become of us?

Brendan C. Boyd and Fred C. Harris

Agganis, a Boston high school and collegiate two-sport legend, was an All-America quarterback at Boston University and a Cleveland Browns first-round draft pick in 1952. But the immensely popular "Golden Greek" stunned pro football by signing with the Red Sox in 1953. After two promising seasons, the first baseman died suddenly, at age 25, of complications following pneumonia.

He charted new dimensions in defensive ineptitude. He dropped foul pop-ups, misplayed grounders, bobbled bunts. He missed pick-off throws, dropped relays, messed up force plays. He fell down while covering the bag on easy rollers, knocked his teammates down while circling under flies. Every ball hit his way was an adventure, the most routine play a fresh challenge to his artlessness. It is hard to describe this to anyone who has not seen it, just as it is hard to describe Xavier Cugat or Allan Ludden.

**Brendan C. Boyd and
Fred C. Harris**

*on the exquisite misplay of
first baseman Dick Stuart
(1963–64)*

Stu once picked up a hot dog wrapper that was blowing toward his first base position. He received a standing ovation from the crowd.

Brendan C. Boyd and
Fred C. Harris
on Dick Stuart

He was one of Boston's own, a kid from Revere who homered into the screen on his first pitch at Fenway as a 19-year-old in 1964. That's something the fans in a city never forget. You break in like that, you're a hero forever.

Carl Yastrzemski
on Tony Conigliaro

Tony C had this funny style of running around the bases after he hit a homer. His head was down, almost as if he was ashamed. Or maybe he didn't want to show up the pitcher.

Carl Yastrzemski
on Tony Conigliaro

The A's need a hit or a Boston mistake. If they are looking for a Boston mistake, I suggest they don't hit it to Remy.

Lon Simmons
Oakland A's broadcaster, 1981, on Boston second baseman Jerry Remy (1978–84)

His repertoire begins with an exaggerated mid-windup pivot, during which he turns his back on the batter and seems to examine the infield directly behind the mound for signs of crabgrass. With men on base, his stretch consists of a succession of minute downward waggles and pauses of the glove, and a menacing sidewise, slit-eyed, Valentino-like gaze over his shoulder at the base runner. The full flower of his art, however, comes during the actual delivery, which is executed with a perfect variety show of accompanying gestures and impersonations.

Roger Angell
sports journalist/author,
on El Tiante, pitcher
Luis Tiant (1971–78)

Tiant is the Fred Astaire of baseball.

Reggie Jackson

The Sox' best pressure hurler between Ruth and Clemens.

Curt Smith
author, on Luis Tiant

There were some left-handed pitchers that had great success there. Bill Lee won 17 games three straight years. Roger Moret. I was never scared of pitching a left-hander in Fenway.

Don Zimmer
manager (1976–80),
coach (1974–76, 1992)

We called him Gentleman Jim, but that was off the field.

Carl Yastrzemski
on pitcher Jim Lonborg

There was a powerful symbolism in Elston Howard coming to Boston. Maybe it would help reverse all those down years. . . . I always thought he was the best catcher I had ever seen for calling a ball game. He could handle pitchers and no one was better at setting up a hitter.

Carl Yastrzemski

Howard, a 13-year veteran of the New York Yankees, was acquired for the Sox' 1967 pennant drive.

Oil Can Boyd flaunted antics that ran counter to self-denial: pumping his arms on K's, pointing at infielders, and stalking in circles around the mound.

Curt Smith
on Boston pitcher
Dennis Boyd (1982–89)

Red Sox fans have surely been blessed; they have had two of the best pitchers in baseball. First they had Clemens, now they have Pedro. The fans really love Pedro. It's his free-caring personality that the fans have been so taken with.

Jerry Remy
on pitching ace
Pedro Martinez

Pedro Martinez

They picked the right guy. He's the best in the business.

Dennis Eckersley

Hall of Fame pitcher
(1978–84, 1998),
on the Red Sox trade for
Pedro Martinez in late 1997

What really catches your eye is how small Pedro is. You go up against Roger Clemens, even if you've never seen him before, and you say, "This guy looks overpowering." You wouldn't say that about Pedro Martinez.

Mark Lemke

nine-year Atlanta Braves
second baseman

I've seen Nolan Ryan at his finest and Roger Clemens at his finest, and Pedro Martinez's control is better than either one. Martinez throws about two or three miles per hour slower than they did, but he throws his breaking ball for strikes more often.

Larry McCoy
American League umpire

If I could play shortstop like him, that's what I would like to do.

Pedro Martinez
on Nomar Garciaparra

[Ken] Griffey's the best, but I'm not sure the shortstop in Boston isn't the second best.

Ted Williams
asked in 1998 who was the top player in the American League, referring to Nomar Garciaparra

He went by all our great players. He had the best rookie year of any player this team ever had.

Dan Duquette
Boston GM (1994–02),
on Nomar Garciaparra,
who topped the AL in hits
(209) and triples (11) and
was second in runs scored
(122) and total bases (365)
—the league's first unani-
mous Rookie of the Year
since Carlton Fisk in 1972

I remember hitting him ground balls in spring training a couple years ago and thinking to myself, *Geez, if this kid was around when I was playing, my butt would be on the bench.*

Johnny Pesky
on Nomar

Nomar Garciaperra

PHOTO COURTESY OF THE BOSTON RED SOX

He combined the best qualities of every Red Sox shortstop in history, displaying Pesky's bat and demeanor, Burleson's arm, Junior Stephens's and Rico Petrocelli's power, and Luis Aparicio's range and speed. He was the rarest of players, particularly for the Red Sox; a five-tool guy.

**Glenn Stout and
Richard A. Johnson**
*authors,
on Nomar Garciaparra*

If only the Red Sox could clone him.

Sports Illustrated
on Nomar

I cannot tell you how many times we've sat there in the dugout and gone, "How the hell did he do that?" He never gets fooled, almost never breaks a bat. He couldn't care less about what a pitcher throws. He figures if it's a strike or anything close to it, he'll hit it.

Lou Merloni
infielder (1998–),
on Nomar Garciaparra

I'm the youngest, Derek [Jeter]'s the richest, and Nomar's the best.

Alex Rodriguez
Texas Rangers shortstop,
before he signed his $248
million deal with Texas,
on baseball's nonpareil
shortstop trio

RED SOX CHARACTER

I'D PITCH THE WHOLE SERIES, every game, if they'd let me.

Babe Ruth

on hurling in the 1918 World Series against the Chicago Cubs, in which Ruth notched two victories and a 1.06 ERA in the Sox' six-game Series triumph

Three hours work on the diamond will start them home about 1:30 o'clock, and they will take the course over the mountains on the return trip. Then the famous Hot Springs baths will follow and, after the usual hour of rest, the boys will be ready to descend full strength upon the dining room.

Edward Barrow
on the 1918 Red Sox spring training regimen in the Ozark Mountains, where the Sox began training in 1909

The "course" refers to a walk of a mile and a half each way from the hotel to the ballpark.

A little more pep, boys, or it's over the mountains on your way home; take your choice.

Edward Barrow

The Boston manager had a built-in motivator at the Red Sox spring training site in Arkansas's Ozark Mountains: Put out in practice or walk the long away back to the hotel.

If they call me [in the World War I U.S. military draft], I am going to make myself efficient at handling the bayonet. You can do great things with one. I will not only practice all day, but after taps I will go to it. You can just tell the world that.

Doc Hoblitzel
first baseman (1914–18)

Red Sox captain in his final year, 1918, Hoblitzel also made the rank of Captain in the U.S. Dental Reserve Corps.

Games were created a long time ago as respites between wars. It's a creative way to use all that energy we have. An art form such as baseball is good, I think, but people get too caught up in the winning and losing because of the economics involved. There's a contradiction there. People come to the park and see a good game, but their team loses and they leave with an empty feeling. They shouldn't. They should enjoy the game for the game's sake. Root, root, root for the home team is fine, but not all this negative booing that goes on. That's what's really wrong with American sports.

Bill Lee
pitcher (1969–78)

If the human body recognized agony and frustration, people would never run marathons, have babies, or play baseball.

Carlton Fisk
*Hall of Fame catcher
(1969, 1971–80)*

I never play by the book because I've never met the guy who wrote it.

Dick Williams
manager (1967–69)

If I was being paid $30,000 a year, the very least I could do was hit .400.

Ted Williams
on hitting .406 in 1941

When you start thinkin' is when you get your ass beat.

Sparky Lyle
pitcher (1967–71)

I don't care who you are, you're gonna be sent down.

Dick Williams
edict to players who weren't hustling

Shooting across that ninth-inning finish by the Red Sox is getting to be just as common as the beans on Saturday night.

Edward F. Martin
The Boston Globe, *April. 1, 1918, after Boston rallied in an exhibition to defeat the Brooklyn Robins (Dodgers) in the ninth inning for the third consecutive time*

He came out of the doghouse and into the guest room more often than my pet Schnauzer. He walked the tightrope of athletic irreverence like a champion.

Ray Fitzgerald
sports journalist,
on Bill Lee

The connection between character and achievement is one of the fundamental fascinations of sport. Some say that sport builds character. Others say that sport reveals character by defeating those who lack it. Wade Boggs reveals his character in the everyday of baseball, by failing fewer times than anyone now playing.

George F. Will
syndicated
columnist/author

He would work out until it was pitch black and we had to kick him off the field. He'd get up before dawn and run a local hill, Snake Hill, dragging a tire. . . . He was an animal, a machine.

Steve Mandl
Manny Ramirez's high school coach, on Ramirez's work ethic

I like it when the pitcher thinks he has given up a hit and, the next thing you know, I'm throwing the guy out. The pitcher gets so excited. You can see it in his face.

Nomar Garciaparra
shortstop (1996–)

There is nothing like seeing a little kid tapping his toes when I'm up at the plate.

Nomar Garciaparra
when asked by a reporter if he considered himself a role model for kids

He's very mature in his work ethic, which gives him consistency. That gives him a chance to be one of the best in the game. More important, he's definitely a solid kid—humble, always open for help. He knows his role and has done very well. I'm happy for him.

Mo Vaughn
first baseman (1991–98), on Nomar Garciaparra

It's refreshing to see a young player with that kind of makeup. This game needs more Nomars.

Paul Molitor
Twenty-one-year major league Hall of Famer, on Nomar Garciaparra

That was better than the Cy Young, better than the new contract. The people mobbed me and hugged me. The priest blessed me. Everyone had tears in their eyes. It was unbelievable.

Pedro Martinez
on visiting a Dominican Republic church built with his monetary contribution
— Sports Illustrated, *1998*

I was watching a game one day when Jason Giambi was talking to him. Giambi called him "Sunshine." That's what he's been. Whenever somebody comes up with something negative, he'll immediately come back with a positive.

John Henry
*Red Sox principal owner
(2002–), on first baseman
Kevin Millar*

RED SOX HUMOR

IN BOSTON, WE BELIEVE . . . the world will break your heart some day, and we are luckier than most—we get ours broken every year, at Fenway Park.

Mordecai Richler
— Expansion, *1979*

One day in September 1923, Babe Ruth lifted a towering fly against the Red Sox. Outfielder Dick Reichle circled under it, but it became obvious that he had lost sight of the ball. By the time the ball landed, Ruth was rounding third and headed for home. When Reichle came to the bench, manager Frank Chance deadpanned, "Pretty smart, Dick. It's late in the season, and I wouldn't get hit on the head either."

David S. Neft, Michael L. Neft, Bob Carroll, and Richard M. Cohen

I still think neckties are designed to get in your soup.

Ted Williams

We were the Mets before there was a Mets.

Carl Yastrzemski
on the Red Sox history of failure

With ballplayers, it's either baseball or sex. It's all physical stuff. But then, we are physical animals; we try to limit our intellectual abilities because it hurts our performance.

Bill Lee

In baseball, you're supposed to sit on your ass, spit tobacco, and nod at stupid things.

Bill Lee

Bill Lee. Another USC man. When they come out of USC, they go directly to the moon.

Lon Simmons
San Francisco Giants announcer

Twenty-five men came to the park, played a ballgame, and took 25 cabs home.

Ron Luciano
umpire,
on the Red Sox of the late 1970s

No lefties, no speed; what's a bunt?

Bill James
*author/historian/senior
advisor, Red Sox baseball
operations,
on the 1981 Red Sox*

If I were a Tibetan priest and ate everything perfect, maybe I'd live to be 105. The way I'm going now, I'll probably only make it to 102. I'll give away three years to beer.

Bill Lee

Not many people talk to you when you're hitting .195.

> **Dwight Evans**
> *right fielder (1972–90),*
> *asked if he ever gets advice*
> *when in a hitting slump*

They all changed. Most of them got agents, and I ceased to talk to 'em. "Like to use this toilet paper?" "Dunno, I gotta talk to my agent."

> **Bill Lee**
> *on today's players*

Being around him made me feel well.

Jimmy Piersall
*outfielder (1950, 1952–58),
on onetime Oakland A's
owner Charles O. Finley*

It's a lot easier when you're starting, because when you're starting you can pick your days to drink.

Bill Lee

He sounds a lot funnier when he's winning.

Dick Williams
on Bill Lee

I met him on the space shuttle.

Lon Simmons
*former Oakland A's
announcer (1981–95),
on Bill Lee*

Sometimes I think I'm in the greatest business in the world. Then you lose four straight and want to change places with the farmer.

Joe McCarthy
manager (1948–50)

The only thing worse than watching the Red Sox is watching them sober.

Anonymous fan
on the banning of alcohol on Good Friday 1998 at Fenway Park

Gaylord Perry has been approached by every investment firm in San Francisco. After all, he's the man who took a 39-cent jar of Vaseline and made himself a $100,000 pitcher.

Bobby Bolin
pitcher (1970–73)

I think one of these days it's gonna happen that the little ground ball that went through Bill Buckner's feet will probably be caught.

Pedro Martinez

Bill Buckner once had a 19-game hitting streak going and always wore the same underwear. Of course, he didn't have any friends.

Lenny Randle

infielder and teammate of Buckner on the 1980 Chicago Cubs

[**M**anny] Ramirez is from another planet. He and Pedro Martinez are probably rooming together on Pluto.

Rick Peterson
Oakland A's pitching coach

Manny is Tom Hanks in *Big*.

Ian O'Connor
journalist, USA Today

THE GREEN MONSTER

IT WAS BUILT to keep baseballs in play, but its beauty is the memory of all the balls that have sailed over it. No one knows when the left-field wall was first called the Green Monster, but it stands upright as the signature feature of this singular baseball park.

Dan Shaughnessy

One of the interesting features of the early Fenway Park was Duffy's Cliff, named after the popular left fielder Duffy Lewis. It was a steep, 10-foot embankment that warned the fielder of an impending crash into the left-field fence. Fans also sat on top of the cliff whenever there was an overflow crowd. It wasn't until 1934 that owner Tom Yawkey removed Duffy's Cliff and erected a 37-foot-high concrete wall that eventually became known as the Green Monster.

**Ty Waterman and
Mel Springer**

It is impossible to overstate what the Wall means to Fenway. It has changed the way the Red Sox play baseball, sometimes saving them, but more often killing them (hello, Bucky Dent). It would be difficult to find another sports arena with a feature as famous as Fenway's Green Monster.

Dan Shaughnessy

Fenway Park is notoriously booby-trapped. In the left-field corner, there is a doorway facing out to the field. When a ball catches the far corner of the doorway, it can carom directly backward, hitting the opposite side of the doorway, which will then bumper-jump the ball to the Wall, where it will take another carom.

David Falkner
author

Our outfielders had trouble there. Don Buford had a ball go through his legs twice in left field. It skipped through once, then he turned around, and it came off the Wall back through his legs again.

Jim Palmer
on a Baltimore Orioles teammate

Inside the scoreboard . . . it's boiling in the summertime and freezing in the spring and fall. But the kids get to talk with opposing left fielders, and Ted Williams says some of his favorite Fenway memories are chats with the faceless, Oz-like men behind the scoreboard.

Dan Shaughnessy

The Wall has scared generations of left-handed pitchers, and rare is the southpaw who will pitch inside at Fenway.

Dan Shaughnessy

Mel Parnell was the last lefty to win twenty games for Boston, in 1953.

Carl Yastrzemski was the master of Wall-ball defense.

Dan Shaughnessy

I loved having that thing behind me.

Carl Yastrzemski

When I first got to Boston, the Wall was cement and then tin. . . . When you had the tin and the rivets, and those two-by-fours every few feet, you never knew where the ball was going to come off. If it hit the two-by-fours, the ball would bounce back just as if it had hit the cement. If it hit the dead spot, it would just drop down. Then it might rattle around the ladder and you'd just have to wait for it to come down. There was nothing you could do.

Carl Yastrzemski

I knew when the ball was going out. It was something I worked into the decoy. But it used to tick the pitchers off. Bill Monbouquette used to say, "Can't you at least make it look like you can catch it?" Meanwhile, the ball would be on its way over the fence to a spot three-quarters of the way out to the railroad tracks.

Carl Yastrzemski

Climbing high into the left-field sky, a deep rich green, the "Monster" hovers over the field. It dominates everything—the ball game as well as the grass and the fans. It's so intimidating that instead of lazily rolling over the ball field, eyes always end up focused on the big green thing out in left.

Bob Wood
author

Children remember the Green Monster the way they remember their first look at the Grand Canyon or the Golden Gate Bridge. Size matters. The Green Monster is impossible to ignore or forget.

Dan Shaughnessy

I've seen fielders go nuts because they just didn't know what to do with the Wall. They'll try to guess where a ball's going to wind up, and instead of going to the ball they'll be standing someplace else looking foolish.

Mike Greenwell
left fielder (1985–96)

Bucky Dent's home run beat the Red Sox in the infamous one-game playoff of 1978, denying the best Boston team of the last half-century its chance to compete in the post-season. It's a cruel joke that a sawed-off shortstop representing the New York Yankees would be the one to use the Wall like no other player in baseball history.

Dan Shaughnessy

Everyone talks about the Wall, but the Wall doesn't mean a thing. People forget about the wind, and it's the wind that really matters. But I don't look for our pitching staff to win the ERA title. You pitch in that park, you're going to give up a few runs.

Al Jackson
pitching coach (1977–79)

Fenway is the "Monster." Like Wrigley's ivy, it just cannot be resisted. While the ivy charms one into a dream state, Boston's great green wall intimidates. Like a mountain range shadowing the short left field, the beast dominates the beauty of the park. Every play in some way is affected by it. Every pitcher throws with the Wall in mind. Every batter swings with its presence felt. . . . The "Monster" remains as dominating to the game today as it was when it first took its lair.

Bob Wood

RED SOX LEGENDS

CAN I THROW HARDER than Joe Wood?
Listen, friend, there's no man alive
who can throw harder than "Smokey
Joe" Wood.

> **Walter Johnson**
> *Washington Senators*
> *Hall of Fame pitcher*
> *(1907–27)*

Babe Ruth started as a pitcher and became an outfielder, but Joe Wood did it first. His switch wasn't dictated by his bat but by a sore arm.

David S. Neft, Michael L. Neft, Bob Carroll, and Richard M. Cohen

on the conversion of one of baseball's legendary flame-throwers to the outfield

Wood pitched for the Red Sox from 1908 to 1915, before being traded to Cleveland in 1917. His once gem of an arm now gone, Wood was switched to the outfield from 1918 to 1922 and hit a fine .298.

I would like to have got a better hold on that one.

Babe Ruth

on his March 24, 1918, spring training blast against the Brooklyn Robins (Dodgers), described by players on both teams as the longest drive they had ever seen.

An account in The Boston Globe *recorded that the smash "cleared the right field wall, but stayed up, soaring over the street and a wide duck pond, finally finding a resting place for itself in a nook of the Ozark hills."*

Babe Ruth was properly Gargantuan, like the eponymous figure from Rabelais. He simply filled out the imaginative space before him.

Michael Seidel
author

I know how to write a ticket on that fellow now. He may say that he is Babe Ruth, but I have another name for him. He is John J. Production, or I miss my guess.

Ed Barrow

The more I see of Babe, the more he seems a figure out of mythology.

Burt Whitman
Boston sportswriter, 1918

Just pipe that swing he takes. I'll admit there were many of those old boys who performed before my time who could whale them, but I never saw a player that could send it on the journey that Babe does, and never did I see any student smash at them so hard.

Johnny Evers
Hall of Fame second baseman, who joined the Sox for spring training in 1918

I was pitching one day, when my glasses clouded up on me. I took them off to polish them. When I looked up at the plate, I saw Jimmie Foxx. The sight of him terrified me so much that I haven't been able to wear glasses since.

Lefty Gomez
New York Yankees pitcher, on the Hall of Famer who played with the Red Sox from 1936 to 1942

Foxx's biceps seemed to carry 35 psi air in them.

Ted Lyons

Even his hair has muscles.

Anonymous pitcher
on Jimmie Foxx

Jimmie Foxx

Lefty Grove

The most impressive thing in spring training was listening to Foxx hit.

Ted Williams

writing home about his first spring training with the Red Sox in 1938

The powerful Foxx's swing made a crushing sound when he connected with the ball. Williams said the only other time in his career that he heard that same sound was when Mickey Mantle first came up.

Lefty Grove could throw a lamb chop past a wolf.

Arthur "Bugs" Baer

cartoonist/sportswriter, on the Hall of Fame pitcher who recorded 105 of his 300 career wins with the Red Sox (1934–41)

Joe Cronin always said that Al Simmons was the best defensive left fielder in the game's history, and he rated Yastrzemski equal. Yaz had been an infielder in the minors, and that's how he played the outfield: charging grounders, flinging strikes to bases.

Curt Gowdy
famed broadcaster and Red Sox radio announcer (1951–65)

Baseball tests your emotional stability. You have to be emotionally identical every day. I'm not talking about myself. I'm thinking of Carl Yastrzemski.

Carlton Fisk

You don't always *make* an out. Sometimes the pitcher *gets* you out.

Carl Yastrzemski

He was never Ted, only Yaz; never celluloid, only calloused flesh.

Peter Gammons
Boston Globe *columnist, current ESPN analyst*

Carl Yastrzemski won't be remembered for a specific hit. . . . Even he listed his greatest memories as his diving stop off Reggie Jackson in the third game of the '75 playoffs, the throw that cut down Bob Allison on October 1, 1967, and the catch off Tom Tresh that kept alive Billy Rohr's no-hit bid that was lost in the ninth but symbolized New England's leap out of the Dark Ages.

Peter Gammons

Carl Yastrzemski

As I stepped out of the box that last time at bat, I tried to look around at every sign and every face to say "thank you" to the people of New England who make this the greatest place to play baseball in the world.

Carl Yastrzemski
on his last day as a player

I swallowed my tobacco both times.

Don Zimmer
manager (1976–80),
on two 500-foot home runs
hit by Jim Rice in 1978

I've never heard a bat louder than his. You hear it going through the strike zone and the sound is unmistakable. It goes *vump*. That's when he misses.

Ken Harrelson
*first baseman/outfielder
(1967–69) and onetime
Red Sox announcer,
on the sound of a Jim Rice
swing*

The "Gold Dust Twins"—rookies Jim Rice and Fred Lynn—flanking right fielder Dwight Evans formed the best Sox outfield since Duffy Lewis, Tris Speaker, and Harry Hooper.

Curt Smith

Watching him hit was like watching a marathoner running alone far ahead of the field. There was nothing compelling about the experience until the end of the race when it was possible to look at the numbers.

**Glenn Stout and
Richard A. Johnson**

*on the subtlety of
Wade Boggs's hitting
accomplishments*

Every game he played he seemed to hit a couple of fifteen-hoppers up the middle for a hit.

**Glenn Stout and
Richard A. Johnson**

on Wade Boggs

You can't play on the Red Sox without someone, every day, bringing up names like Joe Cronin and Ted Williams, and Cy Young.

Mike Greenwell

PHOTO COURTESY OF THE BOSTON RED SOX

Roger Clemens

All the individuals that have won 300 games share the same characteristics—terrific fire, competitive excellence, killer instinct, knowledge of how to win, and knowing what not to do to lose. . . . Roger has a terrific level of concentration, focus, and exceptional work habits, which has led to excellence over a long period of time.

Tom Seaver

Hall of Fame pitcher,
on Roger Clemens

8

SHRINE TO NO. 9

TED WILLIAMS'S CAREER touched upon four great decades of American baseball—from just before World War II through the golden decades of the 1940s and '50s—before the sport was blown out of proportion by extensive television coverage, screwy new rules, divisional play, artificial turf, homogenized ballparks, and by multimillionaire .220 hitters.

Michael Seidel

My, he could hit 'em high. Far, okay, okay, but high was the thing. That's why we biked wherever he played. We wanted Williams to hit one, and we just squealed when he put it up, so far up in the air, and then so far out of the park. And he still hit them that way in the majors.

Ray Boone
*Thirteen-year major league infielder (1948–60),
on growing up in San Diego watching the young Ted Williams*

The Splendid Splinter

Coiling on himself like a barber pole turning around.

> **Donald Hall**
>
> *poet,*
> *on Ted Williams's*
> *batting stance*

We gotta get that camel-gaited kid with rubber wrists.

> **Joe Cronin**
>
> *Hall of Fame Boston short-*
> *stop and manager,*
> *agreeing with Red Sox GM*
> *Eddie Collins at the 1937*
> *winter meetings, on going*
> *after the young Williams*

Moving into the batter's box with a marble you-bet-I-can look, Williams went through the batter's rites of swing, digging a little depression with the toe of his left foot, bouncing up and down and squeezing the handle of the bat until it seemed that sawdust would come out its end.

Bert Randolph Sugar
author/sports journalist

And now Boston knows how England felt when it lost India.

Ed Linn
author,
after Williams's last
career at-bat, home run
number 521

That kid sure murders the potato.

Stan Spence
onetime Williams team-mate on the minor league Minneapolis Millers (1938)

Ted Williams in a sense cultivated his nature as a ballplayer in a way comparable to Ty Cobb, who used his orneriness as a piece of field artillery.

Michael Seidel

Ted Williams was a different kind of heroic presence—a loner, a brooder, a technician whose skill in the batter's box reigned supreme but whose actions elsewhere proved unsettling and perplexing—more pointedly like the Greek warrior Achilles, who spent a fair share of time sulking in his tent, who had difficult relations with the local press, but who hit with extreme authority at home and on the road. No one ever questioned Achilles's will to engage when the power was upon him.

Michael Seidel

Has he seen *me* hit?

> **Ted Williams**
>
> *to Bobby Doerr in 1938 at spring training, when Doerr asked Williams if he had seen the great Jimmie Foxx hit*

Williams's theory of hitting depended on split-second assessments of ordained hitting zones and an almost eerie self-discipline regarding the nature and frequency of his swings. But away from the plate he seemed to swing savagely and wildly at whatever sucker pitches were tossed to him.

Michael Seidel

In golf, you never hear a single boo.

Ted Williams

The pay is great, and the only way you can get hurt playing is by getting struck by lightning.

Ted Williams
on pro golf

He looked like Plastic Man fumbling for loose change.

Michael Seidel
on Williams's occasional muffs in the outfield early in his career

Ted Williams and John Wayne are synonymous. Someone down in spring training once said that John Wayne has spent his whole life playing Ted Williams.

Bill Lee

Take my answers and be glad I'm talking. I never needed anybody. I always had my bat.

Ted Williams
to the press

You buy every newspaper you can get your hands on and spend half your time reading them—just to find someone to get mad at.

Dom DiMaggio

ribbing teammate Ted Williams

Kid, there's only one way for you to become a hitter. Go up to the plate and get mad. Get mad at yourself and mad at the pitcher.

Ted Williams

to young teammate Jimmy Piersall in spring training

I know there are regulars at Fenway who love to hate me. They get more kicks out of giving me the old razzoo than out of watching the game. For them I have nothing but contempt. But I'll tell you something. I actually think I'd be a better ballplayer if I was booed every day. The boos stir me up.

Ted Williams

I hope somebody hits .400 soon. Then people can start pestering that guy with questions about the last guy to hit .400.

Ted Williams
1980

I have one great regret about the time I played. Year after year, when we headed north after spring training, I never stopped off in Greenville to visit Joe Jackson.

Ted Williams

All I want out of life is that when I walk down the street, folks will turn and say: "There goes the greatest hitter who ever lived."

Ted Williams

If he'd just tip his cap once, he could be elected Mayor of Boston in five minutes.

Eddie Collins
Philadelphia Athletics–Chicago White Sox Hall of Fame second baseman and Boston general manager (1933–47), on Williams

Where would you find another like him in a million years?

Curt Gowdy

Hitting was my life.

Ted Williams

9

FAMOUS MOMENTS

IN THE FINAL GAME of the 1912 World Series against the Giants, Harry Hooper went back for a deep fly ball, leaped high, and speared the ball barehanded, falling backward into the stands. The remarkable play saved the Series, allowing the Sox to win in the 10th inning.

**Ty Waterman and
Mel Springer**

In 1915, after hitting only two home runs all season, [Hooper] slugged two round-trippers in the final game of the World Series against the Phillies to provide the ultimate margin of victory. Then, in the 1916 Series against the Dodgers, Harry batted .333 and scored six runs in five games.

**Ty Waterman and
Mel Springer**

On June 23, 1917, Babe Ruth opened a game against Washington by walking the leadoff man. Ruth decided this was the fault of the ump's poor eyesight and said so loudly and profanely. The umpire ordered a shower to cool Ruth's temper, tossing him out of the game. In came Ernie Shore. The runner on first decided to steal a base but was thrown out, and Shore went on to retire the next 26 batters without incident. He has been regarded as having pitched a most unusual perfect game.

David S. Neft, Michael L. Neft, Bob Carroll, and Richard M. Cohen

In September 1935, Boston had the bases loaded, none out, and Joe Cronin up against the Indians. He lined a ball that glanced off third baseman Odell Hale's head and caromed on the fly to Billy Knickerbocker. The shortstop tossed to Roy Hughes on second base for the second out, who then threw to first, completing the triple play.

Curt Smith

On June 16, 1938, Jimmie Foxx became the only American League player to draw six walks in a nine-inning game.

Curt Smith

How far away must one sit to be safe in this park? I didn't even get the ball. They say it bounced a dozen rows higher, but after it hit my head, I was no longer interested.

Joseph A. Boucher

a spectator who, on June 9, 1946, was beaned by Ted Williams's prodigious 502-foot home run into the right-center field bleachers—the longest homer ever recorded at Fenway Park

In 1984 the Red Sox commemorated the feat. Now located in an ocean of green seats—seat 21, row 37, section 42—is a red plastic chair: the Red Seat.

It's hard to believe anybody could hit a ball that far. I know I've never even come close, not even in batting practice. I mean, it's not even down the line. It's in the gap! You can barely see that thing.

Mo Vaughn

*on the Red Seat,
Williams's marker in
Fenway's right-center field
bleachers that commemo-
rates the longest home run
in Red Sox history*

I had the ball in my hand. I hesitated and gave Slaughter six steps. When I saw him, I couldn't have thrown him out with a .22. Nobody paid any attention to him. I couldn't hear anybody. There was too much yelling. It sounded like an ordinary single. I thought he'd hold up at third so late in the game."

Johnny Pesky

on the legendary eighth-inning first-to-home running by the St. Louis Cardinals' Enos Slaughter, in the seventh and deciding game of the 1946 World Series, that gave the Cards the win and the Series

Pesky stood morosely studying Ford Frick's signature on the ball. . . . At length, he turned dreamily, gave a small start of astonishment . . . and then threw in a sudden panic.

Red Smith

legendary sports journalist, on the Pesky–Slaughter play in the final game of the 1946 World Series

I have played the tape again and again, in slow motion and in stop action. I have timed it with a stop-watch. The verdict: If Pesky held the ball, the camera didn't see him do it. . . . The camera shows Pesky taking the throw, whirling to the left, and throwing home in one continuous motion. Catch, wheel, throw.

John B. Holway

author/researcher, on the controversial Pesky-Slaughter play

If they hadn't taken Dom DiMaggio out of the game, I wouldn't have tried to come home.

Enos "Country" Slaughter

on his legendary dash in Game 7 of the 1946 World Series

Bosox center fielder Dom DiMaggio, whose two-run double tied the game in the top of the eighth inning, was hurt sliding into second base and replaced by weak-throwing Leon Culberson.

It was the greatest catch I ever saw in my life.

Billy Rohr

rookie pitcher, on Carl Yastrzemski's bottom-of-the-ninth diving catch at Yankee Stadium in the second game of the 1967 season that preserved, to that point, Rohr's no-hitter

Circumstances tend to make good plays seem even better.

Carl Yastrzemski

after his circus catch of Tom Tresh's liner to deep left to open the bottom of the ninth preserved rookie Billy Rohr's no-hit bid against the New York Yankees in the Yankees' 1967 home opener

Rohr lost his no-hitter with two outs and two strikes, when Elston Howard singled.

The pitch sailed toward Tony's head. . . . He threw his hands up, but that didn't help. The whole park must've heard the crack the ball made as it hit Tony under the left eye. We all ran out as he collapsed in a heap at the plate. "You're going to be okay. It's gonna be fine," Rico Petrocelli kept whispering to him. You could hear Rico from five feet away because the place had gotten so quiet.

Carl Yastrzemski
on the beaning of Tony Conigliaro, Aug. 18, 1967, by California Angels pitcher Jack Hamilton

Though he made a brief, effective comeback a year and half later, Conigliaro never regained his former stature as one of the game's dominating sluggers.

Out of sight! Over the American flag and out of here!

> **Jim Woods**
> *Red Sox announcer,*
> *on Jim Rice's July 17, 1975,*
> *blast that cleared Fenway*
> *Park's center-field back*
> *wall, just the fifth to do so*

And there goes a shot to deep right field! High in the air, and we watch this one go into the upper deck! His third home run of the night as he goes five-for-six with 10 runs batted in!

> **Ned Martin**
> *Red Sox radio/TV*
> *announcer (1967–91),*
> *on Fred Lynn's stunning*
> *performance at Tiger*
> *Stadium, June 19, 1975*

For the 35,205 wedged into misshapen Fenway on the pleasantly cool October evening, and the millions who watched on television, the sixth game of the 1975 World Series will be the standard by which all the future thrillers must be measured.

Sports Illustrated
Nov. 3, 1975

Game 6 of the 1975 Classic has been called "the greatest game in World Series history" and "the greatest game in the Greatest World Series."

G. Richard McKelvey
author

Carbo hits a high drive! Deep center! Home run! Bernie Carbo has hit his second pinch-hit home run of this Series. And the Red Sox have tied it, 6–6.

Curt Gowdy

on Carbo's two-out home run in the bottom of the eighth inning to tie the Cincinnati Reds in Game 6 of the 1975 World Series

Don't you wish you were that strong?

Bernie Carbo

to Cincinnati third baseman Pete Rose, rounding third after hitting his dramatic Game 6 three-run homer in the '75 World Series

Back goes Evans . . . back, back! And—what a grab! Evans made a grab and saved a home run on that one!

Curt Gowdy

on Boston right fielder Dwight Evans's leaping 11th-inning right-field corner catch with a man on, robbing Cincinnati's Joe Morgan of a potential game-winning home run in Game 6 of the '75 World Series

After making the catch, Evans then fired a rocket to first that doubled up the Reds' Ken Griffey and completed an improbable inning-ending double play.

Somehow I got my glove on the ball to catch it and threw to first base to double off the runner and end the inning. I'm sure that [Joe] Morgan's drive would have made the seats if I hadn't caught it, and at that point, it could've been the end for us.

Dwight Evans

on his game-saving catch of Joe Morgan's right-field 11th-inning drive in Game 6 of the 1975 World Series

Can you believe this ballgame?

Pete Rose

Cincinnati Reds, to Carlton Fisk, during the 11th inning of Game 6 in the 1975 World Series, one inning before Fisk's milestone home run

Every little boy who has ever played on a sandlot has dreamed of winning a World Series game with a last at-bat home run. Even better: Do it in front of the rabid fans of the team you grew up rooting for. In short, do what Red Sox catcher Carlton Fisk did at Boston's Fenway Park in Game 6 of the 1975 World Series. . . . A generation later, Fisk's home run remains the ultimate moment in TV sports, not for its drama but because of its sheer beauty—an American dream come true.

TV Guide
"Fifty Greatest TV Moments of All Time," 1998

Carlton Fisk

Everyone in America remembers where he was when Fisk hit his home run.

> **A. Bartlett Giamatti**
> *onetime commissioner of baseball*

The late John Kiley manned the Fenway organ for three decades, and veteran fans still get chills when they remember Kiley's bursting into the "Hallelujah Chorus" after Carlton Fisk's home run off the foul pole in Game 6 of the 1975 World Series.

> **Dan Shaughnessy**

Call it off. Call the seventh game off. Let the World Series stand this way, three games for the Cincinnati Reds and three for the Boston Red Sox.

> **Ray Fitzgerald**
> *columnist,* The Boston Globe,
> *October 22, 1975, following Game 6 of the 1975 World Series*

I thought we should have won that Series in five games. I really did.

> **Carl Yastrzemski**
> *on the '75 World Series*

In six of the seven games, the winning team came from behind. In one of the games, the winning team came from behind twice. In five games, the winning margin was one run. There were two extra-inning games, and two games were settled in the ninth inning. Overall, the games were retied or saw the lead reversed 13 times. No other Series—not even the celebrated Giants–Red Sox thriller of 1912—can match these figures.

Roger Angell
on the 1975 World Series

So baseball's Athens and Troy would be brought together for a 163rd game. "After all that has happened to both teams," Carl Yastrzemski said, "this is probably the only way it should be settled. But I feel sorry that either team must lose. The two best teams in baseball, the greatest rivalry in sports. There should be no loser."

> *Sports Illustrated*
> *on the 1978 American League playoff game between Boston and New York*

Dent's blast was a 306-foot home run over a fence 305 feet away.

> *Boston Evening Globe*

We talked about loving Fenway so much. It's probably the one time I hated Fenway Park, on the Bucky Dent home run.

Carl Yastrzemski

And here they come up at Fenway! A new record! Clemens has set a major league record for strikeouts in a game! Twenty! What a performance by the kid from the University of Texas!

Ned Martin

on the posting of 20 "K" signs in right field in the ninth inning of Roger Clemens's record-breaking 3–1 victory over Seattle, April 29, 1986

I watched perfect games by Catfish Hunter and Mike Witt, but this was the most awesome pitching performance I've ever seen.

John McNamara
after Clemens's first
20-strikeout game

That's as dominating as I've seen a pitcher pitch. I've had Randy Johnson with a fastball and slider be dominant, but Roger was throwing a two-seam fastball, a four-seam fastball, a forkball, and slider. He threw four pitches and moved the ball around.

Tim McClelland
umpire,
at the conclusion of
Clemens's second 20-K
game, September 18, 1996

That baseball game . . . was the best baseball game, the most exciting baseball game, the most competitive baseball game I've ever seen.

John McNamara
*manager (1985–88),
on Game 5 of the 1986
American League
Championship Series,
California Angels vs.
Boston, which the Red Sox
won in 11 innings, 7–6*

Deep to left and Downing goes back! And it's gone! Unbelievable! You're looking at one for the ages here! Astonishing! Anaheim Stadium was one strike away from turning into Fantasyland! And now the Red Sox lead, 6—5!

Al Michaels

*ABC-TV broadcaster,
on Dave Henderson's two-
run ninth-inning homer off
California's Donnie Moore
in Game 5 of the 1986 ALCS*

It was a big hit. It came at the right time. I don't get too many chances to do that.

Dave Henderson

*outfielder (1986–87),
on his dramatic Game 5
ALCS homer against
California in 1986*

Hendu's bases-loaded sacrifice fly won the game for Boston in the 11th inning.

If there was a bathroom on the mound, I'd have used it.

> **Steve Crawford**
> *reliever (1980–82, 1984–87), on his tension-riddled, ninth-inning, bases-loaded relief appearance against California in Game 5 of the 1986 ALCS*

Crawford, entering the game with one away, closed out the inning and later became the game's winning pitcher of record.

Three and two to Mookie Wilson. . . . A little roller up along first . . . behind the bag. . . . It gets through Buckner! Here comes Knight! And the Mets win it!

> **Vin Scully**
> *NBC-TV broadcaster,
> on the most infamous field-
> ing miscue in Red Sox his-
> tory that gave the New York
> Mets new life and a tie at
> three games apiece in the
> 1986 World Series*

The Mets won Game 7, 8–5.

Forty-one years of Red Sox baseball flashed in front of my eyes. In that one moment, Johnny Pesky held the ball, Joe McCarthy lifted Ellis Kinder in Yankee Stadium, Luis Aparicio fell down rounding third, Bill Lee delivered his Leephus pitch to Tony Perez, Darrell Johnson hit for Jim Willoughby, Don Zimmer chose Bobby Sprowl over Luis Tiant, and Bucky (Bleeping) Dent hit the home run.

Peter Gammons
in the immediate aftermath of Buckner's boner

What bothers me the most is the way the media has blown it out of proportion.

Bill Buckner

You knew the ending. You just didn't know how. They are the Red Sox. . . . Just as Hamlet dies every night, the Red Sox die every time they take the stage.

The Baltimore Sun
during the fallout after the 1986 World Series

The 1986 World Series seized the nation like no other in recent years. It was baseball as Americans know and love it—a throbbing, good-God-what's-next World Series that had Americans' hearts pumping in every time zone—the kind of theater that no other sport can generate.

Shirley Povich
columnist,
The Washington Post

10

THE GREAT RED SOX TEAMS

In the early years, the Red Sox almost could not lose at their new home field. The 1912 Red Sox, known as "the Speed Boys" in many accounts, went 57–20 at home and beat the New York Giants in seven games to win the World Series.

Dan Shaughnessy

The crowd was making more noise than any Boston crowd had since the Colonials took two from the British at Concord and Lexington.

Robert W. Creamer
author/sports journalist,
on the 1918 World Series
between the Red Sox and
the Chicago Cubs

A good, but not typical, Sox club. No tattooing the Wall. They just singled and doubled and tripled you to death.

Bobby Doerr
on the 1975 Red Sox

The Sox had always been a folk team throughout New England. Now in the playoff and, especially, Series, people saw what we saw every day—the small park, the depth of fans' knowledge of the game. In other words, baseball like at Ebbets Field or Shibe Park. Baseball like it was meant to be.

Ned Martin
on the 1975 Red Sox

We're the best team in baseball. But not by much.

Sparky Anderson
Cincinnati Reds manager, after the Reds' Game 7 victory over the Red Sox in the 1975 World Series

The Red Sox were favored to repeat as pennant winners in 1947, but they were sideswiped by an incredible outbreak of aching arms. The top three starters from 1946 (Tex Hughson, Dave Ferriss, and Mickey Harris) were all stricken during spring training. The hurlers who had posted a cumulative 62–28 record in 1946 slumped to 29–26. Tragically, none of them ever fully recovered.

**David S. Neft, Michael L.
Neft, Bob Carroll, and
Richard M. Cohen**

The 1948 Red Sox could hit with anyone. The team's 907 runs scored led the league, as did Williams's .369 batting average.

> **David S. Neft, Michael L. Neft, Bob Carroll, and Richard M. Cohen**

Some would contend that the 1949 Red Sox were the best club in team history.

> **Glenn Stout and Richard A. Johnson**

Oh how those Red Sox of the early 1950s could hit!

> **David S. Neft, Michael L. Neft, Bob Carroll, and Richard M. Cohen**

The members of the deservedly winning, champion Reds and of the sorely disappointed, almost-champion Red Sox will in time remember this Series not for its outcome but for the honor of having played in it, for having made it happen.

> **Roger Angell**
> *on the 1975 Red Sox*

We weren't a powerful club, not a lot of home runs, but fate seemed to like us.

> **Joe Castiglione**
> *Red Sox radio announcer,*
> *on the 1986 Bosox*

What can you say? You know what the poets say: "Hope springs eternal in the human breast."

> **John McNamara**
> *on his 1986 Red Sox team*
> *that had just beaten the*
> *California Angels in*
> *Game 7 of the ALCS*

This team has been remarkable all year in our ability to never quit and never give in. That's a testament to everyone in our clubhouse. Everyone has had a hand in helping us win games.

> **Jason Varitek**
> *catcher (1997–),*
> *on the 2003 Red Sox follow-*
> *ing their dramatic 4–3 win*
> *over Oakland in Game 5 of*
> *the American League*
> *Division Series that sent the*
> *Sox to the ALCS*

They are very difficult to pitch to because they have no soft spot. You don't give your pitcher any time off when he goes through that lineup. They don't strike out. They grind out the at-bats.

Joe Torre
New York Yankees manager, on the 2003 Red Sox

11

THE ALL-TIME
RED SOX TEAM

ALL-TIME TEAMS, originally established
to honor the immortals that grace the
great field of play, have been the
occasional first missile fired in the
war on baseball sensibility. Logic and
statistical comparison, those stalwart
pillars of unerring choice, buckle
under the uncertainty of any subjec-
tive process of selection.

Nothing in sports is guaranteed to
marshal the appetites of combative
conversation quicker than the posting

of an all-time team. The timorous and insipid need not apply.

Fortunately, the vast Red Sox landscape is lit by a host of illustrious deities, making certain tenants at certain positions virtually inarguable. While a consensus of acceptance will likely never be a possibility with such an undertaking, it is with the boldness of Joshua and the courage of Daniel that I present the Boston Red Sox All-Time Team.

ALL-TIME RED SOX TEAM

JIMMIE FOXX, *first base*

BOBBY DOERR, *second base*

WADE BOGGS, *third base*

NOMAR GARCIAPARRA, *shortstop*

CARLTON FISK, *catcher*

TED WILLIAMS, *outfield*

CARL YASTRZEMSKI, *outfield*

TRIS SPEAKER, *outfield*

MEL PARNELL, *left-handed pitcher*

ROGER CLEMENS, *right-handed pitcher*

JOE CRONIN, *manager*

Jimmie Foxx could hit a home run over that wall with half a swing.

Bob Feller
Cleveland Indians
Hall of Fame pitcher

JIMMIE FOXX
First base (1936–42)

The powerfully built "Double X" moved over to Fenway in 1936, playing seven seasons through 1942, his legendary status already well secured after an 11-year stint with Connie Mack's Philadelphia Athletics, one of baseball's greatest teams of the late 1920s and early '30s.

Foxx smashed 222 of his career 534 home runs with the Red Sox, good enough for seventh all-time in current club history. He notched his career-best RBI season in 1938, when he led the league with 175, the same year he logged 50 home runs, his second-best season total.

His prodigious strength was said even to awe the usually unimpressionable Ted Williams, who wrote home from his first spring training with the Red Sox that the most impressive thing gained from the experience was listening to the sound of Foxx swinging a bat.

The Herculean first baseman is part of one of baseball's epic milestones—one of five American League sluggers fanned consecutively by Carl Hubbell in the 1934 All-Star Game.

I don't think I've ever met a finer human being in my life than Bobby Doerr.

David Halberstam
Pulitzer Prize-winning author and historian

BOBBY DOERR
Second base (1937–44, 1946–51)

Steady, dependable, quiet, courteous, friendly
. . . Hall of Famer Bobby Doerr sounds more
like a boy scout than the best second baseman in Red Sox history. But his consistent,
reliable manner was the bedrock of the great
Sox teams of the late 1940s, and they recipro-
cated by naming him captain. He even gained
Ted Williams's respect and eventually became
one of the few people Williams trusted.

Doerr jumped to the majors in 1937 after
three sterling seasons in the Pacific Coast
League, moving right into the Red Sox
Opening Day lineup as a starter. By 1940, he
was well on his way to career totals that still
leave him fifth all-time in club annals in RBIs
(1,247), games played, at-bats, runs scored,
doubles, total bases, and extra-base hits. In
addition, Doerr ranks sixth in home runs
(223), hits (2,042), and walks (809).

In 14 seasons in Boston, he was named to
the All-Star Game nine times and was selected
The Sporting News Player of the Year in 1944.
He is the only Red Sox player to hit for the
cycle twice.

He collected base hits like a three-year-old at the beach collects rocks.

**Glenn Stout and
Richard A. Johnson**
on Wade Boggs

WADE BOGGS
Third Base (1982–92)

Initially unheralded even within the Red Sox organization itself, Boggs became baseball's premier hitter of the 1980s during his 11 seasons in Boston.

From 1985 to 1988 he won four consecutive American League batting titles and five times led the loop in on-base percentage. Boggs ranks second all-time to Ted Williams in club annals in career batting average (.338), and his skill at slapping balls off the Wall ultimately left him fourth all-time in doubles (422). He notched 200 or more hits in a season seven straight years, a modern record, and scored 100 or more runs seven consecutive times as well.

Boggs worked hard to improve inconsistent fielding throughout his early career and eventually wound up garnering two Gold Glove Awards, in 1994 and '95.

The man known as "Chicken Man"—a phrase coined by teammate Jim Rice regarding Boggs's preference for fowl—was an 11-time all-star and registered his 3,000th base hit, a home run, in 1999 with Tampa Bay in his 18th and final season.

If I could have any one player and were starting a team, I'd start it with Garciaparra.

Bill Lajoie

Red Sox special assistant to the general manager/ scouting (2003–), when he was with the Atlanta Braves organization

NOMAR GARCIAPARRA
Shortstop (1996–)

Nomar, universally regarded as one of the game's three current best shortstops, has all-time credentials after just seven seasons with Boston. He became only the sixth player in history to be unanimously selected American League Rookie of the Year, when he debuted in 1997 with a league-leading 209 hits and 11 triples.

Garciaparra won his second consecutive AL batting title in 2000 and had the distinction of hitting the 10,000th Red Sox franchise home run in July of that same year. The five-time all-star became the first player in major league history to hit three home runs in back-to-back innings in an eight-RBI appearance against Tampa Bay on July 23, 2002. He also set the major league record for most doubles by a shortstop (56) and became the fastest Red Sox player to reach 1,000 career hits—all in 2002.

With his skillful play, both offensively and defensively, the sky would seem to pose no limit to Garciaparra's potential lifetime marks should he remain in Boston for the duration of his career.

You don't *play* baseball. You are involved in it, you work at it.

Carlton Fisk

You think you're ready. It sounded all right in the bathroom. It sounded all right in front of the mirror. It sounded all right in the garage. But, wow, is it different once you get up there. It's like taking batting practice. You can take all you want, but that doesn't prepare you to face Randy Johnson, Tom Seaver, or Bob Gibson. It gives you groundwork, but that's all.

Carlton Fisk

on stepping up to the podium for his Hall of Fame induction in 2000

CARLTON FISK
Catcher (1969, 1971–80)

No one moment is more deeply ingrained in Red Sox lore than Fisk's dramatic "stay fair" home run in the 12th inning of Game 6 of the 1975 World Series against the Cincinnati Reds. His game-winning shot tied the Series at three games apiece, catapulting Fisk to near-immortal status.

His debut season in 1972 was punctuated with unprecedented emphasis, when he became the first player in American League history to unanimously win the Rookie of the Year Award.

By career's end, after 11 seasons in Boston and 13 with the Chicago White Sox, Fisk had eclipsed Johnny Bench's all-time mark for most home runs by a catcher, with 351. Along with Bench and Yogi Berra, he is one of only three backstops in major league history to club more than 300 homers, score more than 1,000 runs, and tally more than 1,000 RBIs. He closed out his career as the White Sox' all-time home run leader, with 214.

Fisk was a seven-time all-star with the Red Sox, starting four midsummer classics, and in 2000 became the 13th catcher to be inducted into the Hall of Fame in Cooperstown.

In 1955 there were 77,263,127 male American human beings. And every one of them in his heart of hearts would have given two arms, a leg, and his collection of Davy Crockett iron-ons to be Teddy Ballgame.

Brendan C. Boyd and Fred C. Harris

TED WILLIAMS
Outfield (1939–42, 1946–60)

The nicknames in themselves are legendary: The Kid, the Splendid Splinter, the Thumper, Teddy Ballgame . . .

Ted Williams stands as one of the game's lofty immortals, an icon who many believe was the best hitter in the long history of the game. That's a mouthful, but there is a warehouse full of documentation to support it.

His epic claim to fame is his .406 batting average in 1941, the last man to hit .400 for a season. Williams's passel of records includes tallying the highest on-base percentage of all time (.483). At 39, in 1957, he became the oldest player ever to win a batting title, when he posted his career second-best average of .388. He followed that with another amazing campaign the next year, claiming the batting crown at age 40. In all, Williams won four home run titles and six batting crowns, registering a lifetime batting average of .344. Twice he won baseball's Triple Crown. One can only imagine the career numbers he would have posted had not five years been lost to military service in his prime.

His exit was a classic: home run number 521 in his last at-bat.

If ever a player in baseball history . . . ever had a two-week clutch production to equal Yastrzemski, let the historians bring him forth.

> **Harold Kaese**
> The Boston Globe,
> *on Yastrzemski's .523 batting average, 16 RBIs, 14 runs scored, and five home runs during the final 12 games of the 1967 season*

I knew this was my time and I grabbed it.

> **Carl Yastrzemski**
> *on the final month of his 1967 Triple Crown season*

CARL YASTRZEMSKI
Outfield (1961–83)

The pages of sports history are filled with the efforts of successors attempting to fill the gigantic shoes of immortal predecessors. Most fail, few succeed.

Though it took seven seasons for Carl Yastrzemski to answer the call to become the next Ted Williams in left field for Boston, Yaz left no doubters after his prodigious Triple Crown year of 1967. Potential and promise had been replaced by production and fulfillment.

No one in the legacy of great left fielders at Fenway ever played the Wall as well as Yastrzemski, who seemed to intuit its many quirks and subtleties, like an attentive parent anticipating a problem child's behavior. Yaz and the Wall were one, and his seven Gold Glove Awards are proof.

His majestic career totals, including first all-time in club RBIs, games played, at-bats, runs, hits, doubles, total bases, and extra-base hits, easily ensured his enshrinement at Cooperstown in 1989. In addition, Yaz also holds the odd distinction of being the first Little Leaguer ever inducted into the Hall of Fame.

To say that Tris Speaker revolutionized outfield play wouldn't be quite right because the suggestion would be that the famed Grey Eagle set a pattern. The fact is, he didn't. He broke the mold. Neither before nor since has an outfielder played so shallowly as Speaker did in the course of nearly 22 big-league seasons.

Bob Broeg
The Sporting News

TRIS SPEAKER
Outfield (1907–15)

I hear the fire coming from the camps of Evans, Rice, Hooper, Jensen, DiMaggio, and Greenwell, in what is without doubt the toughest all-time Bosox position to fill, Ted and Yaz being givens.

To get bogged down in a statistical comparison of Speaker and Evans is to become mired in the differences between eras and tenures. Both were outstanding in the field, and had Speaker played 19 seasons in Boston, à la Evans, before being traded in his prime to Cleveland, he likely would have posted numbers of Evans's caliber.

For someone who had to pay his own way to a spring training tryout early in his pro career, the heights came quickly for the man baseball would call the Grey Eagle. Speaker spoke reams, both with his pioneering fielding skills as well as at the plate. As the accompanying quote attests, Speaker carved his own unique niche in the field, his trademark the shallow position in center field, daring batters to try to hit one over his head. Speaker logged a .337 lifetime batting average with the Sox, and his total of stolen bases (267) ranks second all-time in Boston annals.

If there is such a thing as a natural in baseball, it was Mel Parnell. He threw, both teammates and opponents thought, so effortlessly that it was almost unbelievable.

David Halberstam

It was said that Hank Bauer and Mickey Mantle broke so many of their bats against him on sliders coming in on the narrow part of the bat that they felt he should buy them new ones.

David Halberstam
on Mel Parnell

MEL PARNELL
Left-handed pitcher (1947–56)

The most fearsome challenge in Fenway faces the left-handed pitcher. Visitors must deal with the short left-field fence only a few times each season, but for Bosox southpaw Mel Parnell, it was home. Indeed, home sweet home.

Parnell never feared the Wall, amassing a brilliant 71–30 record in 10 seasons at Fenway Park, where the mean Green Monster bites lefties the hardest. Parnell accumulated a 123–75 career record, tops all-time in Red Sox history among left-handers. In 1949, he registered his best seasonal mark, posting a fine 25–7 record with a gleaming 2.77 ERA. His pinnacle moment came in 1956, his final season, when he tossed a no-hitter against the White Sox.

Red Sox history buffs will recall Parnell at the center of controversy just before the 1948 American League playoff game against Cleveland. Boston manager Joe McCarthy made the fateful choice to go with 14-year journeyman Denny Galehouse, an 8–8 pitcher, for the crucial game, passing over Parnell, who had thrown effectively at Fenway all season and was 15–8. The Indians clobbered Galehouse and went on to win the World Series.

Roger's my type of pitcher. . . . He's a pitcher that I would pay to go and see pitch.

Gaylord Perry
*Hall of Fame pitcher,
on Roger Clemens*

It's never in the past. This town, this ballpark, are a part of me. I worked here. I gave my all here. That's the bottom line. That will never change.

Roger Clemens
*on his years with the
Red Sox*

ROGER CLEMENS
Right-handed pitcher (1984–96)

Nearly every milestone associated with a Hall of Fame career and status as a future legend Roger Clemens has accomplished.

The Rocket registered almost two-thirds of his career victories in Boston, tying Cy Young for most wins in franchise history and posting two classic performances that put him in the record book: the pair of 20-K gems tossed a decade apart (1986, '96). He also captured the Cy Young Award an unprecedented six times (three with the Red Sox), more than any other hurler in major league history, and was the American League MVP in 1986.

Believed washed up at 34 after the 1996 season, Clemens was sent to Toronto, where he gained a sweet measure of revenge, claiming two consecutive Cy Youngs in his only two seasons north of the border, before adding a sixth with archrival New York in 2001.

During 13 years in Boston, he recorded more than 200 strikeouts in a season eight times, seven of them consecutively (1986–92). He is the American League's all-time strikeout king (4,099).

In his 50-year career in baseball, Joe Cronin went from shortstop to manager to general manager to American League president. All that, and he was sold to the Red Sox by his wife's uncle.

Steve Richards
The Boston Globe

Washington Senators owner Clark Griffith sold his young all-star shortstop to Boston in 1934 for $225,000, the largest sum in baseball history to that time.

JOE CRONIN
Manager (1935–47)

If there is a Mr. Red Sox based on all-around contribution to the organization, it would have to be Hall of Famer Joe Cronin, who was an all-star shortstop, manager, and general manager during his tenure in Boston. But there was even more ahead for Cronin, who ascended to the American League presidency in 1959 and later was named league chairman (1974).

The AL MVP in 1930 as a 23-year-old shortstop for the Washington Senators, Cronin became player-manager of the Senators at 26—the Boy Manager—and carried them to the World Series in 1933, where they lost to the Giants in five games. He had the curious distinction of being sold by his father-in-law, Senators owner Clark Griffith, to Boston for the then-record sum of $225,000 after the 1934 season. He assumed joint responsibilities with the Sox, again as player-manager, from 1935 through '45.

In 1946, his first year as full-time manager, he led the Red Sox to their first American League pennant in 28 years. Cronin tops all Boston managers in wins, with 1,071. He headed the Boston front office from 1948 to 1958.

RETIRED RED SOX NUMBERS

1 **BOBBY DOERR**, *second base* (1937–44, 1946–51)

4 **JOE CRONIN**, *shortstop/manager* (1935–47)

8 **CARL YASTRZEMSKI**, *left field* (1961–83)

9 **TED WILLIAMS**, *left field* (1939–42, 1946–60)

27 **CARLTON FISK**, *catcher* (1969, 1971–80)

12

FIELDS
OF PLAY

AS I GROW OLDER, I think of Fenway, and I think of everybody wearing a jacket, a tie, a boater, and maybe who Babe Ruth is going to pitch against.

David Halberstam

The Red Sox did not always play their home games at Fenway Park. Boston's charter American League franchise was formed in 1901, and the Huntington Grounds served quite nicely for the first 11 years of its history.

Dan Shaughnessy

Fenway Park was . . . opened in 1912 with a seating capacity of about 27,000—one of the larger ballparks of that era. There was a single-deck grandstand with a right-field pavilion and large wooden bleachers in right and center fields. The left-field fence was 321 feet from home plate, the center-field fence 488 feet away, and the right-field fence only 313 feet. During this dead-ball era, it was extremely rare for anyone to hit the ball over the fence. Only 14 home runs were hit by the Red Sox in 1917, a typical year.

**Ty Waterman and
Mel Springer**

The park's first American League game was scheduled for April 18, but rain pushed it back to April 20. By that time not many people cared. The *Titanic* had gone down on April 15, and the *Carpathia* arrived in New York with survivors the day before the game.

Dan Shaughnessy

The spirit of Babe Ruth has rumbled in historic Fenway Park like the Loch Ness monster . . . ever since the World Series of 1918, when Ruth won two games. But his departure cast a spell that festered in the crevices and eaves of Fenway. In the dark of night at the park, the lonely, haunted spirit of the Red Sox howls.

George Vecsey

I love the idea of Fenway, of a connection to the past. When you go there, you're watching where people watched Babe Ruth pitch, where DiMaggio and Williams had their epic battles. It's where Jimmie Foxx and Ellis Kinder and Mel Parnell had their great seasons. I like it when the past reverberates in our lives.

David Halberstam

Fenway Park is a lyric little bandbox of a ball park. Everything is painted green and seems in curiously sharp focus, like the inside of an old-fashioned peeping-type Easter egg.

John Updike
*Pulitzer Prize-winning
novelist*

Fenway Park is New England's tribal meeting place . . . where members congregate, then leave to savor and debate.

Curt Smith

Fenway Park is a friendly neighborhood joint, the corner bar of American sports palaces.

Dan Shaughnessy

It's no more possible to overdo the finer attributes of Fenway than it is to overdo discussion of the Sistine Chapel or Beethoven's Fifth. Surely what one is to art and the other is to music, Fenway is to ballparks.

Dan Riley

I think the appeal of Fenway Park is that, like life, it's unfair.

George F. Will

Fenway becomes like a piece of furniture in your household. It's as if you've got a couch that may be a little bit old and torn in places, but it's comfortable and familiar, and it's got a lot of memories.

Doris Kearns Goodwin
historian/Pulitzer Prize-winning author

It's important to me and my extended family that my grandfather is known as the builder of the ballpark which is so prominent in the history of baseball. In the family records, we have a picture of Charles Logue with John Taylor, the Red Sox owner, and the Comiskey brothers, visiting from Chicago, at the Opening Day luncheon. However, the game was rained out.

John I. Logue
grandson of Charles Logue,
who built Fenway Park

You should enter a ballpark the way you enter a church.

Bill Lee

A nice ballpark is a really wonderful thing. And it's so nice to be able to walk to it or take a trolley. I think walking up to Fenway is thrilling. The approach to it. The smells. You go to Fenway and you revert to your childhood.

David Halberstam

I take some weird comfort in the knowledge that these poles are the same poles that blocked the vision of my dad and his dad when they would take the trolley in from Cambridge to watch the Red Sox in the 1920s.

Dan Shaughnessy

Recipe for Fenway grass: 85 percent Kentucky bluegrass, 15 percent perennial rye grass, lots of water, lots of love, and keep the fans off the field.

Joe Mooney
Fenway Park
groundskeeper

Fenway was like a home to me. It sure was. I was there as long and as often and as much as anybody that I ever knew. I used to go early and get out late.

Ted Williams

It's like being in an English theater. You're right on top of the stage. So chummy.

Tip O'Neill
former U.S. House Speaker,
born in 1912, the same year
Fenway opened

I don't know anything about classical music, but if there's a baseball symphony, this is it.

Buck Showalter
manager, Texas Rangers

Fenway is a place where you can sit for hours and feel a serenity that does not exist anywhere else in the world.

Anonymous
found in Philip Lowry's
Green Cathedrals

The closeness of the seats in Fenway is what I liked the best.

Carl Yastrzemski

I like the old guys that wipe off your seat. They seem like they were there when the club came in. I love all the little nooks and crannies and places to go—the idea that there's a scoreboard and somebody's behind it, putting up numbers. There's no place like it, and it's ours.

Stephen King
on Fenway

Accept Yankee Stadium as baseball's most famous park; Wrigley Field as its most beautiful; Ebbets Field, revered; and Camden Yards, visionary. Between Carlton Fisk and Bill Buckner, Fenway became its most beloved.

Curt Smith

I'm glad they're going to change Fenway. I think the park has hurt the game some. I've seen a lot of wonderfully pitched ball games there get screwed up because some little pop fly hits up against that fence.

Ted Williams

If you're just talking about pitching, Fenway's not good. . . . I think you have to be a power pitcher to pitch there for a long time. You cannot be a finesse pitcher. Put Greg Maddux in this son-of-a-bitch and let's see what he can do.

Dennis Eckersley

Blow the damn place up.

Mo Vaughn

I want Boston to have the best. If any city needed a new ballpark, they need it. I won't shed a tear. Take a lot of good pictures of it.

Ted Williams

Nowhere else is the park's old and new mix more obvious than in the way it keeps score. Two boards do the job. Each is as different from the other as the Old North Church from the Prudential Building.

Bob Wood

The big thing about Fenway is the crowd. When you come out of that bullpen, it's kind of weird. It's like in the days of the Romans in the Colosseum.

Dennis Eckersley

Fenway's right-field line features a yellow foul pole stationed a hideous 302 feet from home plate. It is affectionately known as Pesky's Pole, named after the lovable Sox shortstop who claims to have curled eight of his 17 career homers inside it.

Dan Shaughnessy

Johnny Pesky logged more than 200 hits a year in his first three seasons with the Red Sox, leading the American League in 1942, '46, and '47.

In the cold weather the ball doesn't carry that well, but in warm weather Fenway Park is a hitter's heaven.

David Ortiz

first base/designated hitter (2003–)

It's the only place I ever pitched where the fans stood up on every fly ball because of the closeness of the fences.

Jim Palmer

I don't think you over-romanticize Fenway Park, but you have to say there's a point at which romance ends. . . . It really requires an act of mature judgment on the part of Red Sox fans. Would they rather lose in a jewel or win in a rhinestone?

George F. Will

I won't be one of those thousands of Save Fenway zealots, hugging the brick walls and lying down in front of bulldozers, but before Fenway is gone I plan to spend some time in the empty yard, remembering.

Dan Shaughnessy

When we lose Fenway, we lose the sense that somebody sat here and watched Ted Williams hit. Somebody sat here and watched Jimmie Foxx and Lefty Grove and Babe Ruth. There's something to be said for that.

Bob Costas
broadcaster

I think you have to get older to appreciate things like Fenway.

Dennis Eckersley

When they raze Fenway, it'll be like cutting down an old tree. Count the rings. There's one for each celebration and heartache suffered by Red Sox fans.

Dan Shaughnessy

Let me get this straight: We're bulldozing real vintage ballparks like Tiger Stadium and Fenway Park to put up fake vintage ballparks?

Rick Reilly
Sports Illustrated

13

DAMN YANKEES

THE BOSTON–NEW YORK RIVALRY

TO CLAIM ALLEGIANCE to the Red Sox, in the same breath you must admit with every ounce of sinew to hold the Yankees in the very utmost contempt.

Bob Wood

All literary men are Red Sox fans. To be a Yankee fan in literary society is to endanger your life.

> **John Cheever**
> *award-winning novelist, 1978*

There's an inherent inferiority complex in Boston. People are bred to hate New York in general terms. It manifests itself most in baseball.

> **Bob Ryan**
> The Boston Globe

Of all New Yorkers, no single soul is more despised than George Steinbrenner. To Bostonians he is the Darth Vader of baseball. From the major league script he's removed poetry, leaving instead debits and credits. . . . Roaming mercenaries, a different set it seems each season, carry out his evil deeds.

Bob Wood
on the Yankees'
owner

This is probably the best rivalry in sports, certainly one of the top two or three. That's why we are so wary of dealing with each other. The summer is always better when the Red Sox are good and the Yankees are good.

George Steinbrenner

Over the years the two teams had historical connections: the Babe hit his first homer against the Yankees, Ted Williams his first hit, my 3000th. The Yankees in 1949 also stopped Dom DiMaggio's 34-game hitting streak—the longest in the American League since brother Joe's 56-game record in 1941. Joe had broken Willie Keeler's record of 44 against Boston. Lou Gehrig's first homer came against the Sox. And then there were the Williams–DiMaggio stories: how Joe beat out Ted for the MVP Award in 1941, even though Ted batted .406.

Carl Yastrzemski

What if Harry Frazee, too dully human to recognize the great gift granted him by the gods that was Babe Ruth, had not sold the wondrous Bambino down the slime river to the loathsome New York Yankees? In doing so, of course, he insulted the gods to such a degree that a curse has been visited upon the Sox from that day forward, resulting in an endless series of ennobling but ultimately futile ascents to the pinnacle of the baseball world.

Dan Riley

The won-lost records never told you anything about the Yankees–Red Sox. It was a rivalry almost of cultures— the New Englanders against the New Yorkers. For us and our fans, it was one of frustration that made hating the Yankees so easy.

Carl Yastrzemski

There is nostalgia here, sure, but it's not the same grass, it's not the same players. You think those old players, Ruth and Williams, you think they ran on this grass? No way. Fenway probably has the same urinals, though. That's about the only thing that hasn't changed. They're the same troughs that guys were using in the old days.

George Steinbrenner

Tommy Henrich, the Yankees' "Old Reliable," always maintained that the reason New York won pennants and the Red Sox didn't was that Tom Yawkey paid his players too well.

> **David S. Neft, Michael L. Neft, Bob Carroll, and Richard M. Cohen**

Throw in your little left fielder, Berra.

> **Tom Yawkey**
> *Red Sox owner (1933–76), to New York Yankees owner Dan Topping, when the two entered into discussion in 1947 about swapping Ted Williams for Joe DiMaggio*

The deal killer came when Yawkey asked for Yogi Berra, not then a top-flight star, in addition to the Yankee Clipper.

It was an insurance run, so I hit it to the Prudential Building.

Reggie Jackson
on hitting one of his home runs in Boston

I'm just tired of seeing New York always win.

Manny Ramirez

We're a select group chosen to break heads. Last week I wrestled a guy down and hit him in the mouth with the best punch I ever nailed a fan . . . don't get me wrong, he was wearing a Yankee hat.

Fenway Park bleacher usher

The Dent homer. I remember like it was yesterday. Usually in October at Fenway, the wind would be blowing in. It would be cool. On that day it was warm and the wind was drifting out a little. . . . When Dent hit that ball, I said, "Good, that's an out." Then I saw Yaz going back, and when he turned around, I said, "Well, that ain't so bad, it's off the Wall." Then the ball went in the net.

Don Zimmer

Everybody knows where they were when I hit the home run. It's something because of the magnitude of the Red Sox history and the Yankee history, our catching them on the last day. There was so much riding on that game. It was a special day. One of those things that doesn't come along very often.

Bucky Dent

People that saw that game, or were there, or part of it, I don't think they'll get over it until they actually win a World Series, and then they can get rid of the old memories.

Bucky Dent

I remember when Lou Piniella made that save in the sun. That was the play of the game. It was a great game. No matter who won or who lost.

George Steinbrenner
*on the 1978 one-game
playoff at Fenway between
New York and Boston*

You can't be on the Red Sox for very long before the sad history is brought up to you. Sure, the Sox have had great teams over the years, and great players. But the Yankees were the ones who took what could have been our greatest years away from us.

Carl Yastrzemski

It's been said before, but it's true: For Red Sox fans, watching Roger Clemens thrive as a Yankee is the equivalent of watching your ex-wife marry your sworn mortal enemy—then live happily ever after.

Sean McAdam
sportswriter

If this could be the World Series, it should be the World Series. Every three-game series between these two teams is like the World Series. I don't think it can get any better than this.

Kevin Millar
first baseman (2003–),
on the eve of the 2003
American League
Championship Series

With Pedro Martinez pitching against Roger Clemens, we all anticipated a great afternoon in the storied Yankees–Red Sox rivalry, but no one expected *The Jerry Springer Show* to break out.

Jim Caple
sportswriter,
on the Game 3 disturbances
of the 2003 ALCS between
Boston and New York

Andy Pettitte and I went over there, and I saw a bald head on the ground.

Roger Clemens

on the volatile eruption in the fourth inning of Game 3 of the 2003 ALCS, when New York coach Don Zimmer went at Pedro Martinez and was thrown to the ground

THE
CLUBHOUSE

WHEN THE NEW UNIFORMS reach the team this spring, the players will all be required to make a deposit, for the Boston management has decided to put a stop to the mysterious disappearance of sweaters and uniforms each fall.

Paul H. Shannon

reporter,
The Boston Post,
March 24, 1918

When I'm through, I'll wind up face-down in the Charles River.

Bill Lee

I'd be the laughingstock of baseball if I changed the best left-hander in the game into an outfielder.

Edward Barrow
on Babe Ruth, 1918

Most managers are lifetime .220 hitters. For years, pitchers have been getting those managers out 75 percent of the time, and that's why they don't like us.

Bill Lee

All managers are losers. They are the most expendable pieces of furniture on earth.

> **Ted Williams**
> *just prior to becoming manager of the Washington Senators in 1969*

Spitball pitching proved to be just the tonic that the Old Family Physician prescribed for the Red Sox today. They laced the Robins 10–4, whacking moist chuckers Dan Grimer and Larry Cheney for 20 blows.

> **Edward F. Martin**
> The Boston Globe,
> *April 5, 1918*

I can remember the clubhouse. We had little wire seats and little folding chairs.

Ted Williams

No question that Dick Williams was the right man for us in 1967. His attitude helped turn around a team and brought the Sox a sense of accountability. He was wrong, though, in ripping guys in public and in keeping them in his doghouse. The day he was fired, I hit two homers and drove in four runs against the Yankees.

Carl Yastrzemski

The clubhouse was rough . . . but it was Fenway. It was cramped, but you know what? When you're talking about clubhouse chemistry and being together, there's nothing like the locker room in Fenway Park.

Jim Palmer

All I've ever done for Boston was give 100 percent and constructively criticize them when I thought they needed it. That's the way I am. I'm their conscience. I'm Jiminy Cricket.

Bill Lee

You must never interrupt the pitcher's focus by talking to him before a start, even if he's just reading the latest issue of *Hustler* or watching the early edition of *SportsCenter*. Instead, avoid any contact with him, regarding him with the same caution you would a psycho killer, a disgruntled postal worker, or Roger Clemens.

Jim Caple

The best show on television is Red Sox baseball. Everything else sucks.

Stephen King

Reverse the Curse. Go Sox!

Anonymous fan's sign
*at Fenway Park during
Boston's 5–4 win over
Oakland in Game 4 of the
2003 American League
Division Series*

What can't you believe? This has been happening for 80 years now. If they ever win—that's something you can't believe.

Mike O'Neil
*Red Sox fan,
after Game 7 of the 2003
ALCS loss to the Yankees*

15

WORLD SERIES LINEUPS

THE HEADLINERS WHO STRODE Fenway's stage during the Red Sox' pinnacle but all-too-rare October moments are always remembered—Collins, Wood, Speaker, Williams, Yastrzemski, Fisk, Doerr, Tiant, Boggs, Rice. But the fabric of a pennant winner also gathers the forgotten ones who toil in silence—Hoblitzel, Stahl, Cady, Gardiner, York, Andrews, Barrett, Owen. All bore the Boston banner in the Fall Classic.

THE 1903 RED SOX
91–47
Jimmy Collins, *manager*

Jimmy Collins, *third base*

Lou Criger, *catcher*

Bill Dinneen, *pitcher*

Patsy Dougherty, *left field*

Duke Farrell, pinch hitter

Hobe Ferris, *second base*

Buck Freeman, *right field*

Tom Hughes, *pitcher*

Candy LaChance, *first base*

Jack O'Brien, *pinch hitter*

Fred Parent, *shortstop*

Jake Stahl, *center field*

Cy Young, *pitcher*

Starting lineups in **bold**

THE 1912 RED SOX
105–47
Jake Stahl, *manager*

Neal Ball, *pinch hitter*

Hugh Bedient, pitcher

Forrest "Hick" Cady, *catcher*

Bill Carrigan, *catcher*

Ray Collins, *pitcher*

Clyde Engle, *pinch hitter*

Larry Gardner, *third base*

Charley Hall, *pitcher*

Olaf Henriksen, *pinch runner/pinch hitter*

Harry Hooper, *right field*

Duffy Lewis, *left field*

Buck O'Brien, *pitcher*

Tris Speaker, *center field*

Jake Stahl, *first base*

Heinie Wagner, *shortstop*

"Smokey Joe" Wood, *pitcher*

Steve Yerkes, *second base*

THE 1915 RED SOX
101–50
Bill Carrigan, *manager*

Jack Barry, *second base*
Forrest "Hick" Cady, *catcher*
Bill Carrigan, *catcher*
Rube Foster, *pitcher*
Del Gainer, *pinch hitter*
Larry Gardner, *third base*
Olaf Henriksen, *pinch hitter*
Dick Hoblitzel, *first base*
Harry Hooper, *right field*
Hal Janvrin, *shortstop*
Dutch Leonard, *pitcher*
Duffy Lewis, *left field*
Babe Ruth, *pinch hitter*
Everett Scott, *shortstop*
Ernie Shore, *pitcher*
Tris Speaker, *center field*
Pinch Thomas, *catcher*

THE 1916 RED SOX
91–63

Bill Carrigan, *manager*

Forrest "Hick" Cady, *catcher*
Bill Carrigan, *catcher*
Rube Foster, *pitcher*
Del Gainer, *pinch hitter*
Larry Gardner, *third base*
Olaf Henriksen, *pinch hitter*
Dick Hoblitzel, *first base*
Harry Hooper, *right field*
Hal Janvrin, *second base*
Dutch Leonard, *pitcher*
Duffy Lewis, *left field*
Carl Mays, *pitcher*
Mike McNally, *pinch runner*
Babe Ruth, *pitcher*
Everett Scott, *shortstop*
Ernie Shore, *pitcher*
Chick Shorten, *center field*
Pinch Thomas, *catcher*
Tilly Walker, *center field*
Jimmy Walsh, *center field*

THE 1918 RED SOX
75–51
Edward G. Barrow, *manager*

Sam Agnew, *catcher*

Joe Bush, *pitcher*

Jean Dubuc, *pinch hitter*

Harry Hooper, *right field*

Sam Jones, *pitcher*

Carl Mays, *pitcher*

Stuffy McInnis, *first base*

Hack Miller, *pinch hitter*

Babe Ruth, *pitcher/outfield*

Wally Schang, *pinch hitter/catcher*

Everett Scott, *shortstop*

Dave Shean, *second base*

Amos Strunk, *center field*

Fred Thomas, *third base*

George Whiteman, *left field*

THE 1946 RED SOX
104–50

Joe Cronin, *manager*

Jim Bagby, *pitcher*
Mace Brown, *pitcher*
Paul Campbell, *pinch runner*
Leon Culberson, *outfield*
Dom DiMaggio, *center field*
Joe Dobson, *pitcher*
Bobby Doerr, *second base*
Clem Dreisewerd, *pitcher*
Dave Ferriss, *pitcher*
Don Gutteridge, *second base*
Mickey Harris, *pitcher*
Pinky Higgins, *third base*
Tex Hughson, *pitcher*
Earl Johnson, *pitcher*
Bob Klinger, *pitcher*
Tom McBride, *right field*
George "Catfish" Metkovich, *pinch hitter*
Wally Moses, *right field*
Roy Partee, *catcher*
Johnny Pesky, *shortstop*
Glen "Rip" Russell, *third base*
Mike Ryba, *pitcher*
Hal Wagner, *catcher*
Ted Williams, *left field*
Rudy York, *first base*
Bill Zuber, *pitcher*

THE 1967 RED SOX

92–70

Dick Williams, *manager*

Jerry Adair, *second base*
Mike Andrews, *second base*
Gary Bell, *pitcher*
Ken Brett, *pitcher*
Joe Foy, *third base*
Russ Gibson, *catcher*
Ken "Hawk" Harrelson, *right field*
Elston Howard, *catcher*
Dalton Jones, *third base*
Jim Lonborg, *pitcher*
Dave Morehead, *pitcher*
Dan Osinski, *pitcher*
Rico Petrocelli, *shortstop*
Mike Ryan, *catcher*
Jose Santiago, *pitcher*
George Scott, *first base*
Norm Siebern, *right field*
Reggie Smith, *center field*
Lee Stange, *pitcher*
Jerry Stephenson, *pitcher*
Jose Tartabull, *center field*
George Thomas, *right field*
Gary Waslewski, *pitcher*
John Wyatt, *pitcher*
Carl Yastrzemski, *left field*

THE 1975 RED SOX
95–65

Darrell Johnson, *manager*

Juan Beniquez, *left field*
Rick Burleson, *shortstop*
Jim Burton, *pitcher*
Bernie Carbo, *pinch hitter/left field*
Reggie Cleveland, *pitcher*
Cecil Cooper, *first base*
Denny Doyle, *second base*
Dick Drago, *pitcher*
Dwight Evans, *right field*
Carlton Fisk, *catcher*
Doug Griffin, *pinch hitter*
Bill Lee, *pitcher*
Fred Lynn, *center field*
Rick Miller, *left field*
Bob Montgomery, *pinch hitter*
Roger Moret, *pitcher*
Rico Petrocelli, *third base*
Dick, *pitcher*
Diego Segui, *pitcher*
Luis Tiant, *pitcher*
Jim Willoughby, *pitcher*
Rick Wise, *pitcher*
Carl Yastrzemski, *left field/first base*

THE 1986 RED SOX
95–66
John McNamara, *manager*

Tony Armas, *pinch hitter*
Marty Barrett, *second base*
Don Baylor, *designated hitter*
Wade Boggs, *third base*
Dennis "Oil Can" Boyd, *pitcher*
Bill Buckner, *first base*
Roger Clemens, *pitcher*
Steve Crawford, *pitcher*
Dwight Evans, *right field*
Rich Gedman, *catcher*
Mike Greenwell, *pinch hitter*
Dave Henderson, *center field*
Bruce Hurst, *pitcher*
Al Nipper, *pitcher*
Spike Owen, *shortstop*
Jim Rice, *left field*
Ed Romero, *shortstop*
Joe Sambito, *pitcher*
Calvin Schiraldi, *pitcher*
Bob Stanley, *pitcher*
Dave Stapleton, *first base*

16

RED SOX AWARD WINNERS

I HANDED THE HICKOK BELT, as America's top professional athlete for 1967, over to Mr. Yawkey. He kept it in a display case in his office, along with a silver bat that Ted Williams had given him. I want the Hickok Belt in the Hall of Fame now, but with a plaque under it that will tell the public I had given it to Mr. Yawkey, so they'll understand the affection I had for him.

Carl Yastrzemski

RED SOX AMERICAN LEAGUE MVPs

(voted by the Baseball Writers
Association of America)

1912   **Tris Speaker**, *center field* *

1938   **Jimmie Foxx**, *first base*

1946   **Ted Williams**, *left field*

1949   **Ted Williams**, *left field*

1958   **Jackie Jensen**, *right field*

1967   **Carl Yastrzemski**, *left field*

1975   **Fred Lynn**, *center field*

1978   **Jim Rice**, *left field-designated hitter*

1986   **Roger Clemens**, *pitcher*

1995   **Mo Vaughn**, *first base*

* *Award officially called the Chalmers Award from 1910 to
1914*

RED SOX CY YOUNG
AWARD WINNERS

1967 **Jim Lonborg**

1986 **Roger Clemens** *

1987 **Roger Clemens**

1991 **Roger Clemens**

1999 **Pedro Martinez**

2000 **Pedro Martinez** *

* Unanimous selection

RED SOX AMERICAN LEAGUE ROOKIES OF THE YEAR

(voted by the Baseball Writers Association of America)

1950 **Walt Dropo**, *first base*

1961 **Don Schwall**, *pitcher*

1972 **Carlton Fisk**, *catcher* *

1975 **Fred Lynn**, *center field*

1997 **Nomar Garciaparra**, *shortstop* *

* *Unanimous selection*

BIBLIOGRAPHY

Bayles, Fred. "Red Sox fans know this feeling very well." *USA Today*. 17 October 2003: 4C.

Boswell, John and David Fisher. *Fenway Park: A Stadium Pop-Up Book*. Boston: Little, Brown and Company, 1992.

Boswell, Thomas. *How Life Imitates the World Series*. New York: Penguin Books, 1982.

Bresciani, Dick and the Boston Red Sox publications and archives departments. *2003 Boston Red Sox Media Guide*. Boston, 2003.

Chieger, Bob. *Voices of Baseball*. New York: Atheneum, 1983.

Falkner, David. *Nine Sides of the Diamond*. New York: Random House, 1990.

Halberstam, David. *Summer of '49*. New York: William Morrow and Co., Inc., 1989.

Honig, Donald. *The Boston Red Sox: An Illustrated Tribute*. New York: St. Martins Press, 1984.

Kaufman, Louis and Barbara Fitzgerald, Tom Sewell. *Moe Berg: Athlete Scholar Spy*. Boston: Little, Brown and Company, 1974.

McKelvey, G. Richard. *Fisk's Homer, Willie's Catch and the Shot Heard Round the World*. Jefferson, North Carolina: McFarland & Company, Inc., 1998.

National Baseball Hall of Fame and Museum, Inc., the National Baseball Library and Gerald Astor. *The Baseball Hall of Fame 50th Anniversary Book*. New York: Prentice Hall Press, 1988.

Neft, David S. et al. *The Boston Red Sox Fan Book*. New York: St. Martin's Griffin, 2002.

O'Connor, Ian. "Manny, we hardly know you, but who does? Your high school coach." *USA Today*, 10 October 2003: 2C.

Riley, Dan, ed. *The Red Sox Reader*. Thousand Oaks, Calif.: Ventura Arts, 1987.

Ross, Alan. *Echoes from the Ball Park*. Nashville, TN: Walnut Grove Press, 1999.

Seidel, Michael. *Ted Williams: A Baseball Life*. Chicago: Contemporary Books, Inc., 1991.

Shaughnessy, Dan and Stan Grossfeld. *Fenway: A Biography in Words and Pictures*. Boston: Houghton Mifflin Company, 1999.

Smith, Curt. *Our House*. Lincolnwood, IL: Masters Press, 1999.

Stout, Glenn and Richard A. Johnson. *Red Sox Century*. Boston: Houghton Mifflin Company, 2000.

Sugar, Bert Randolph. *Baseball's 50 Greatest Games*. New York: Exeter Books, 1986.

Thorn, John et al. *Total Baseball: The Official Encyclopedia of Major League Baseball*, Fifth Edition. New York: Viking Penguin, 1997.

Tuite, James, "Sports World Specials" *The New York Times*, 29 March 1978: C2.

Walton, Ed. *This Date in Boston Red Sox History*. New York: Stein and Day, 1978.

Waterman, Ty and Mel Springer. *The Year the Red Sox Won the Series*. Boston: Northeastern University Press, 1999.

Williams, Ted and John Underwood. *The Science of Hitting*. New York: Simon and Schuster, 1971.

Wood, Bob. *Dodger Dogs to Fenway Franks*. New York: McGraw-Hill Book Company, 1988.

Yastrzemski, Carl and Gerald Eskenazi. *Yaz*. New York: Doubleday, 1990.

Web Sites:

www.soxland.homestead.com/quotes.html

www.baseball-almanac.com/quotes/
roger_clemens_quotes.shtml

www.baseball-almanac.com/quotes/
quoclls.shtml

www.baseballhalloffame.org/news/300wins.htm

www.pedroplace.homestead.com/quotes.html

www.brainyquote.com/quotes/quotes/n/
nomargarci104221.html

www.geocities.com/Colosseum/Track/4242/
quotes.htm

INDEX